D0591588

empty pockets

A collection of stories produced by the students of
P. Gloeckner's narrative art course at the University of Michigan
School of Art & Design, funded for the most part by student lab fees.

Design: Alisa Bischoff

The Wooden Book Press

Post Office Box 7664, Ann Arbor, MI 48107
www.woodenbook.org

ISBN: 0-9769020-0-1
Printed in the United States of America

First Printing, May 2005

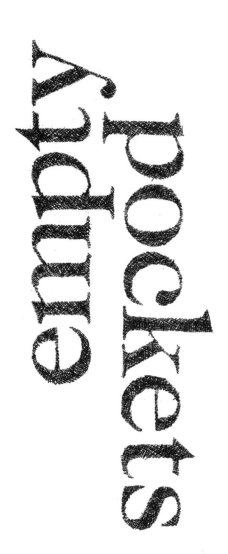

empty pockets

contents

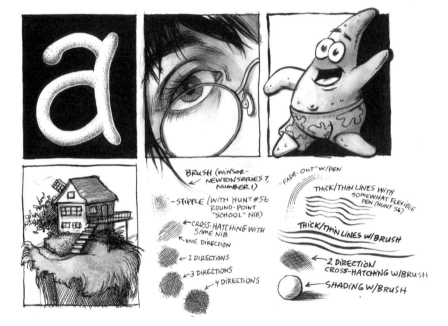

The following text labels appear within the drawing exercise:

BRUSH (WINSOR-NEWTON SERIES 7, NUMBER 1)

-STIPPLE (WITH HUNT #56 ROUND-POINT "SCHOOL" NIB)

CROSS-HATCHING WITH SAME NIB

ONE DIRECTION

2 DIRECTIONS

3 DIRECTIONS

4 DIRECTIONS

"FADE-OUT" W/PEN

THICK/THIN LINES WITH SOMEWHAT FLEXIBLE PEN (HUNT 56)

THICK/THIN LINES W/BRUSH

2 DIRECTION CROSS-HATCHING W/BRUSH

SHADING W/BRUSH

A drawing exercise by Professor Gloeckner for class demonstration.
Apologies to Patrick Star and the Spongebob people.

preface

University of Michigan, Ann Arbor
School of Art and Design
May 3, 2005 (Tuesday, 9:53PM)

Dear Reader,

The book you hold represents the efforts of 37 fledgling artists, all of them students in my "narrative art," "graphic novel," or "comics" class—words are not adequate to describe what we set out to do.

The students came with all levels of experience, many of them burdened with prejudices about what comics are or should be nearly as unshakable as my own.

Somehow, together, we nonetheless reached this delicious moment—tomorrow, this book, with its dizzying variety of style and subject matter, goes to the printer.

To you, dear students—please know that I'm proud of you all. And thanks—you helped make my first year @ the U of M rich and challenging, and not in the least bit slittious.

Yours most sincerely,
Professor Gloeckner

Jessica Yurasek • Eli L. Adam & His Quest To Become Hobo King

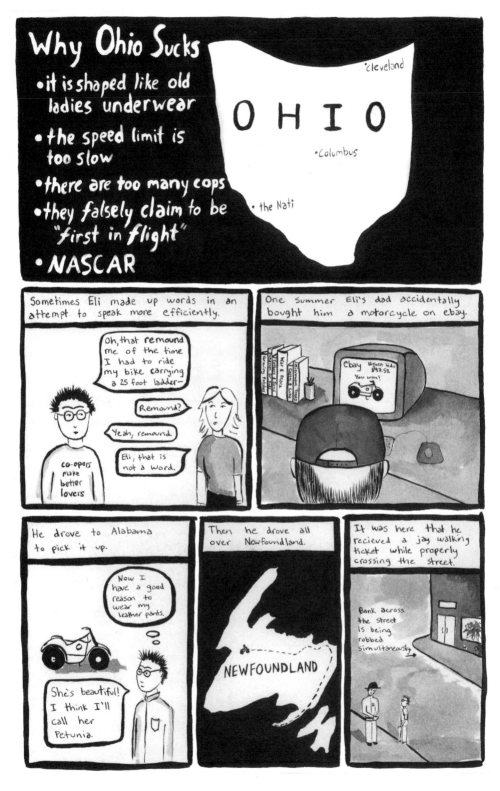

When he returned from his travels, Eli grew bored.

He began to wander the countryside following the train tracks in search of tin cans.

One night he visited my house wearing a cape he sewed out of torn pillowcases and socks.

Standing on an old milk crate, he recited his pretend Hobo King acceptance speech.

Greetings fellow hobos. We are gathered here today to give thanks. I want to thank you for this opportunity to reign. I also want to tell you about my dream. I have a dream that one day, I will be able to push a cart of coke bottles around many towns with a whip. The whip's purpose would be to snap imposter cokes out of the fooled people's hands and immediately after toss a beautiful red, cold coke into their stinging digits. I picture my rightful distribution get-up as including a cape, but you probably already figured that much. Now, with your support, this dream can be realized.

Hey, Sylvia...

Do you think this coffee can makes me look fat?

Geoff the Geow by Geoffrey Silverstein

Geoff the Geow by Geoffrey Silverstein

Jim Gianpetro • First Day Of School

Jim Gianpetro • First Day Of School

25

Jessie Howell • Photo Not Available

For 30 years antidepressants have con
in two basic varieties: tricyclics (such
and Tofranil) and monoamine oxidase
or MAOIs (Nardil, Parnate). No one
quite ho
depress
feature
seroton

AUTHOR'S NOTE PROZAC WAS
RELEASED BY ELI LILLY IN 1987 --
BY 1990 PRESS COVERAGE WAS
AT AN ALL-TIME HIGH. SALES
WENT FROM $125 MILLION IN 1988 TO
$350 MILLION IN 1990. IT WAS
HAILED AS A MIRACLE DRUG - JH.

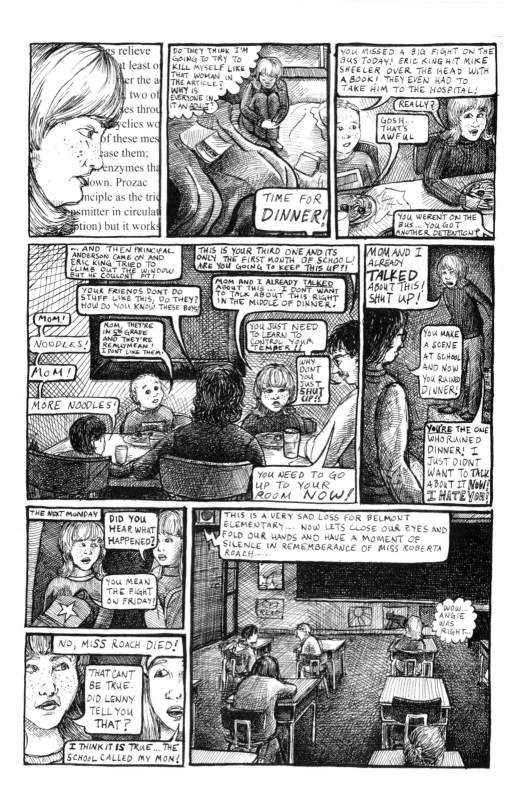

Jessie Howell • Photo Not Available

29

Jessie Howell • Photo Not Available

Seagull Island • Sarah Sutton

WORLD DOMINATION

They talk, they think. They're going to take over the world.

I know some of you are skeptical but our training facilities have proved that with our scavenging and shrill voices we've already been able to take out most of the upper peninsula. Obviously no one has noticed.

We will attack in 3 days.

3:00:00

Start arming yourselves and start eating only green leaves. The key to this war is going to be deadly shit.

Oh my God, look at all those guns!

I've got to get back to tell the police.

oh no. seagulls.

that was close.

33

Seagull Island • Sarah Sutton

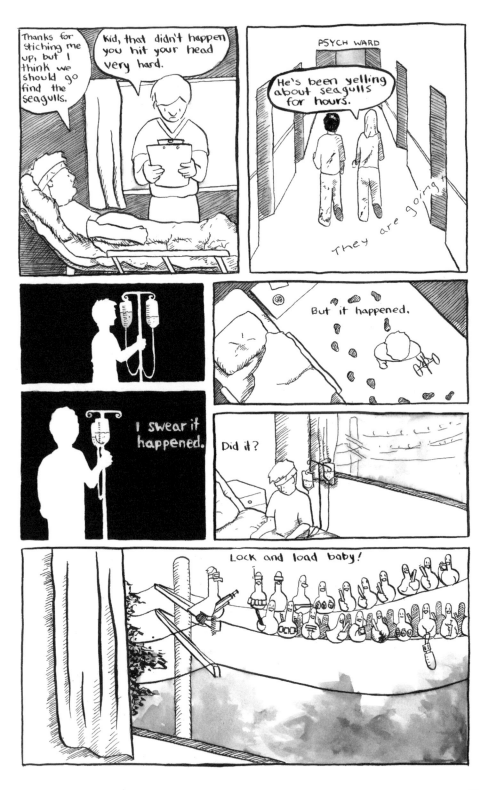

35

The History Lesson • Sam Butler

The History Lesson • Sam Butler

Often times I would lay and listen to music. Daydreaming about the day I would get my Powers.

It all seemed so BAD ASS.

I would go to school and show Everyone. Things like:

How I could shape-shift into whatever or whoever I wanted.

OR Fly anywhere at super fast speeds...

OR Run so fast you could barely see my legs...

OR Even be a telepath and read people's minds, or lift objects just by thinking about it.

Catholicism vs. Comics • Cristina Mezuk

Catholicism vs. Comics • Cristina Mezuk

So... why are you crying?

Well...*snif* it's kind of complicated...

My mom did make me feel better, and a little silly. But I couldn't shake my feeling of betrayal...

Are you going to go to Sunday School today?

Naw..

So naturally I wound up losing a lot of faith in God...

Regardless of how Ridiculous my wishes were.

I mean, c'mon... Shaq?

wee!

Oh well...

But I was a kid who put a lot of faith into something, and it came up waaay short. I just wish he had listened to me a wee bit.

Catholicism vs. Comics by Cristina Mezuk

Made In Manga • Lia Min

(note: "right on")

Made In Manga • Lia Min

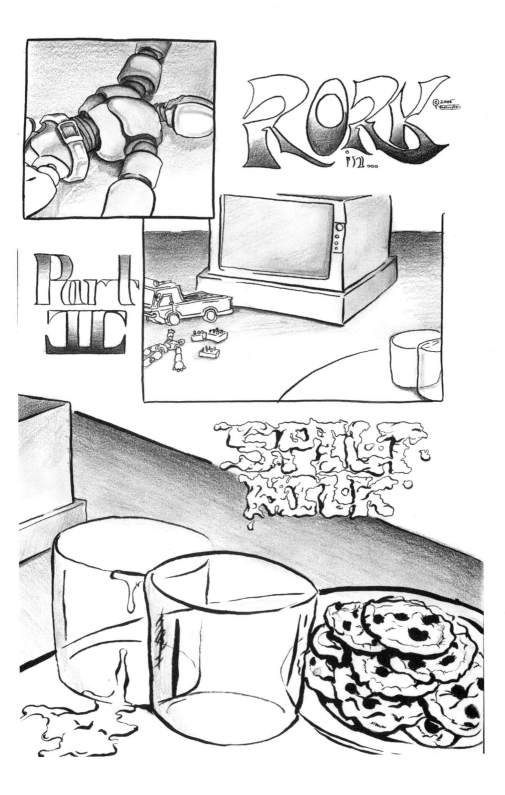

Little Nancy Thunder • Max Jaksa

Little Nancy Thunder • Max Jaksa

Old Tread • Zach Takenaga

71

Old Tread • Zach Takenaga

73

It started off like any other lonely night...

Broken Pistol • Jonathan Ho

Broken Pistol • Jonathan Ho

81

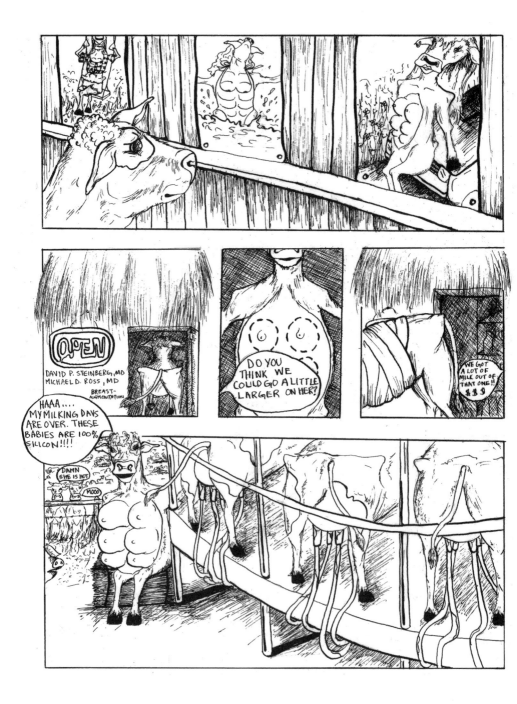

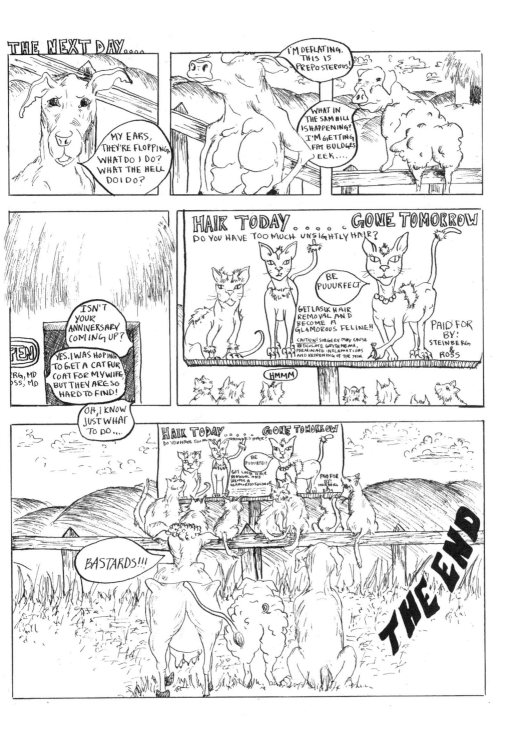

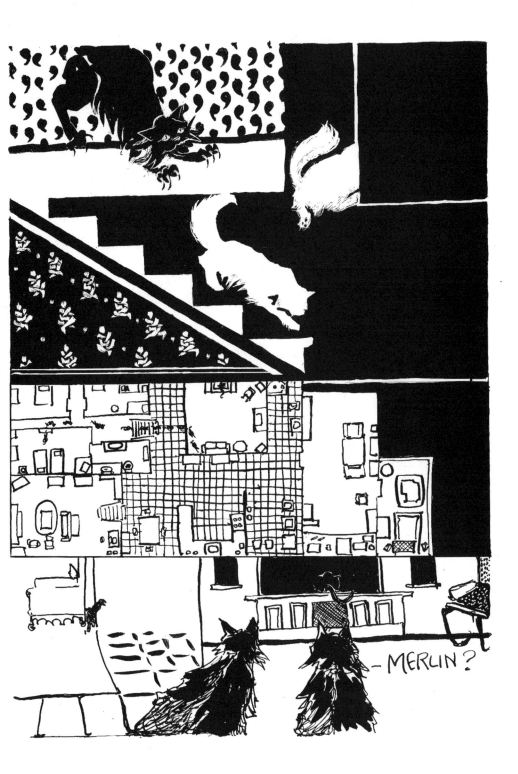

Nearly 30 Years • Angela Stork

SO, WHAT'S WRONG WITH THAT?
WELL THEY DIDN'T USED TO. THEY HAD ONE BIG BED AND THEY SLEPT WITH THEIR HEADS NEXT TO EACH OTHER.
WHAT DOES DIVORCE MEAN? I HEARD THEM YELLING IT THE OTHER NIGHT.
I DON'T KNOW ROSINI. LET'S GO OUTSIDE.
OK!

A Second Chance? • Jessie Howell

93

A Second Chance? • Jessie Howell

95

Cars • Kevin O'Neill

Cars • Kevin O'Neill

Cars • Kevin O'Neill

Ladies Night at the PINK FLAMINGO

MEGHAN JONIEC

Ladies Night At The Pink Flamingo • Meghan Joniec

103

Ladies Night At The Pink Flamingo • Meghan Joniec

Ladies Night At The Pink Flamingo • Meghan Joniec

Welcome To Stapleton • Alisa Bischoff

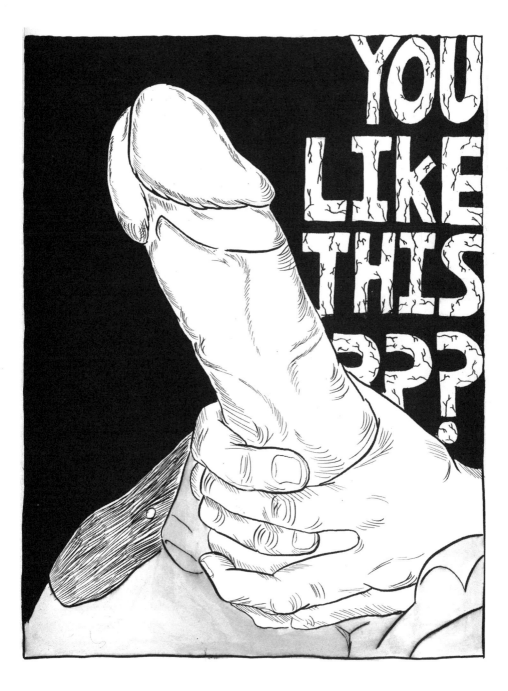

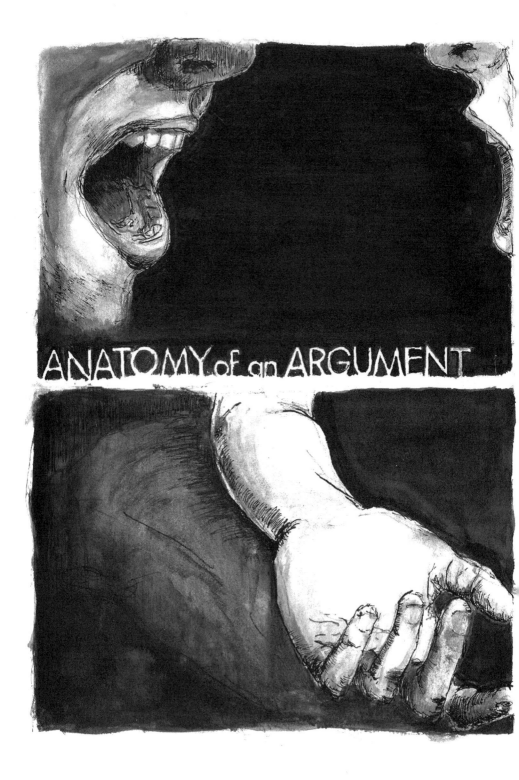

Alexis Jakobson • Anatomy Of An Argument

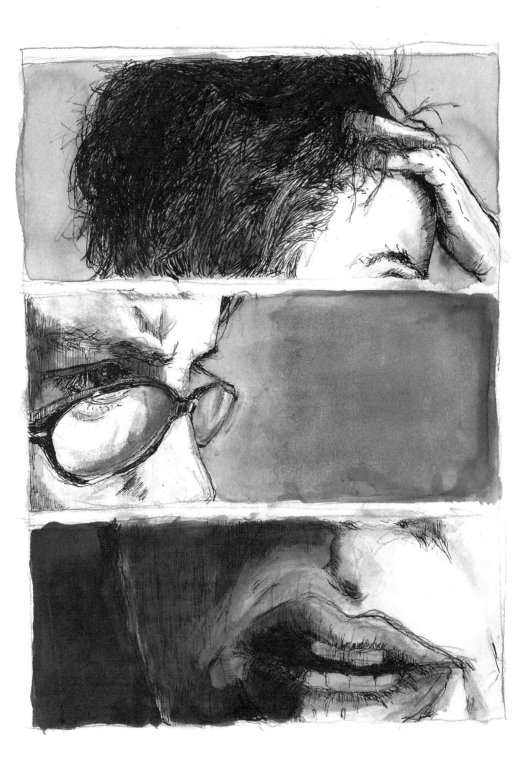

Alexis Jakobson • Anatomy Of An Argument

Alexis Jakobson • Anatomy Of An Argument

THE LONG DAYS of SUMMER

Kelly Campbell

Kelly Campbell • The Long Days Of Summer

Kelly Campbell • The Long Days Of Summer

Kelly Campbell • The Long Days Of Summer

Kelly Campbell • The Long Days Of Summer

131

Tabula Selenographica • Jeremy Stoll

133

Grandpa • Sarah Sutton

137

Grandpa • Sarah Sutton

Grandpa • Sarah Sutton

Even though Dad doesn't believe me I know what kind of man you are.

Being old is not an excuse.

One Boring Friday • Patrick Eckhold

147

A Man walks in the dark.

What does he bury?

Tell me a story.

I only have sad stories to tell.

On a camping trip, scary stories would do.

What will I bury?

Horror stories are also sad stories. They admit the truths that can't be said outright. Death is real. The murder of dreams is real. Every day terrible things happen, such that it tears our world. Ghosts are just the imprint of the atrocity.

A mother throws her unwanted child into the flames of the fireplace.

A woman sees a rotten thing at her window in the night. "A vampire", she says. The men put a stake through the leper's heart.

People die, or kill to end the pain their lives have become.

LOVEDEATH • Bruce Brenneise

151

LOVEDEATH • Bruce Brenneise

155

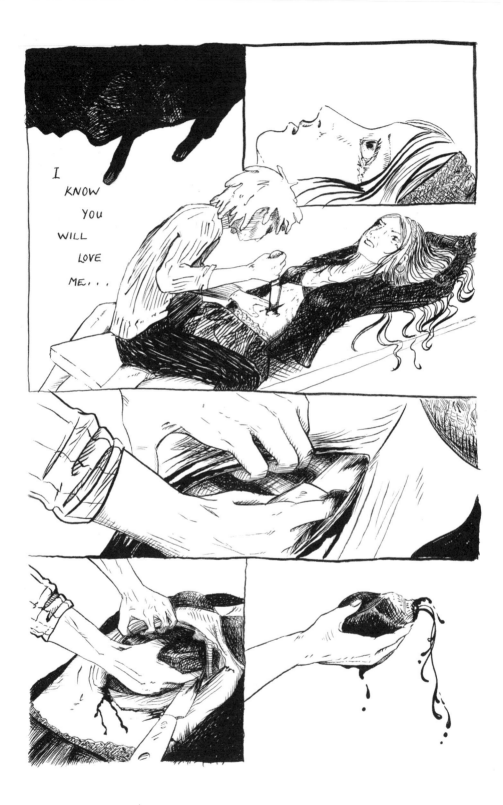

We All Scream For Ice Cream • David Tesnar

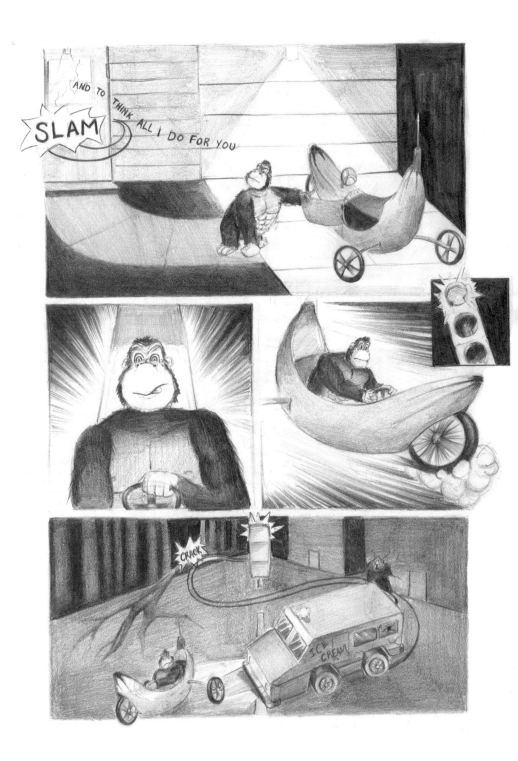

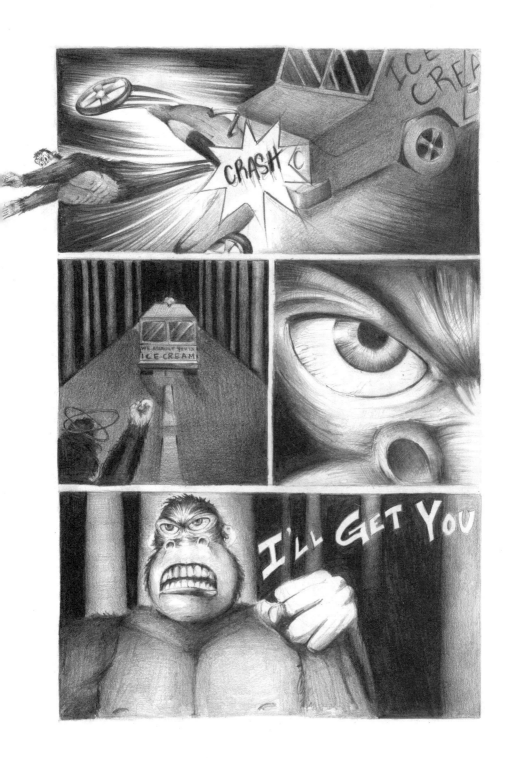

We All Scream For Ice Cream • David Tesnar

163

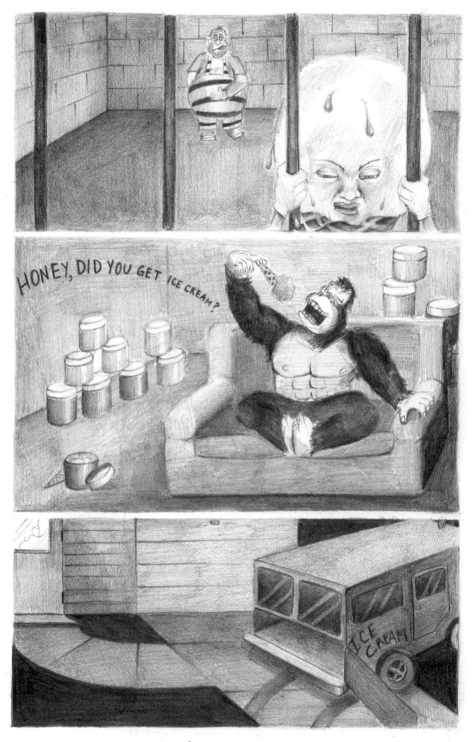

ALL DONE

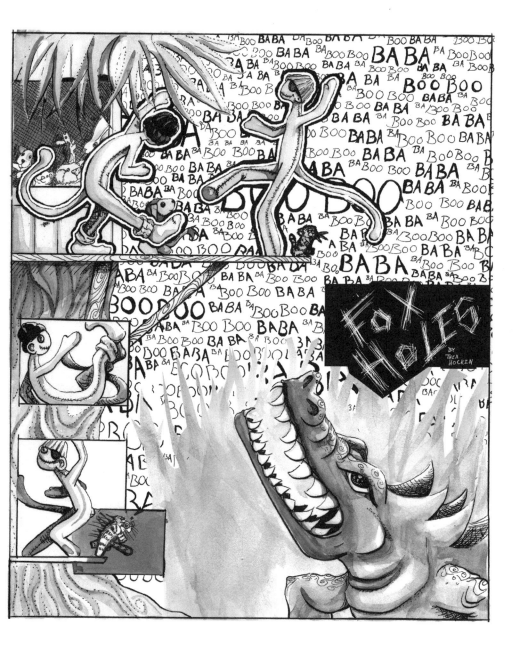

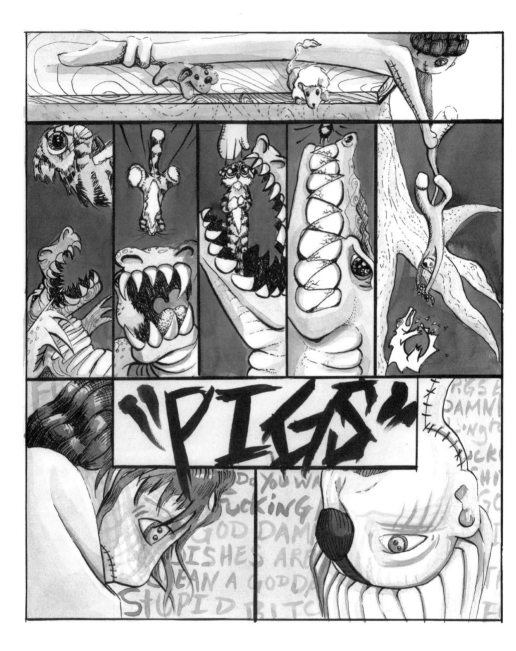

Fox Holes • Thea Hockin

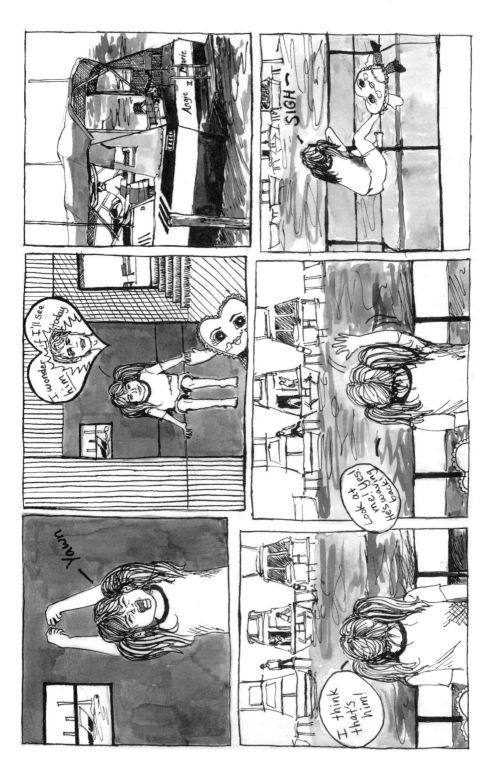

I Got My Mind Set On You • Angela Stork

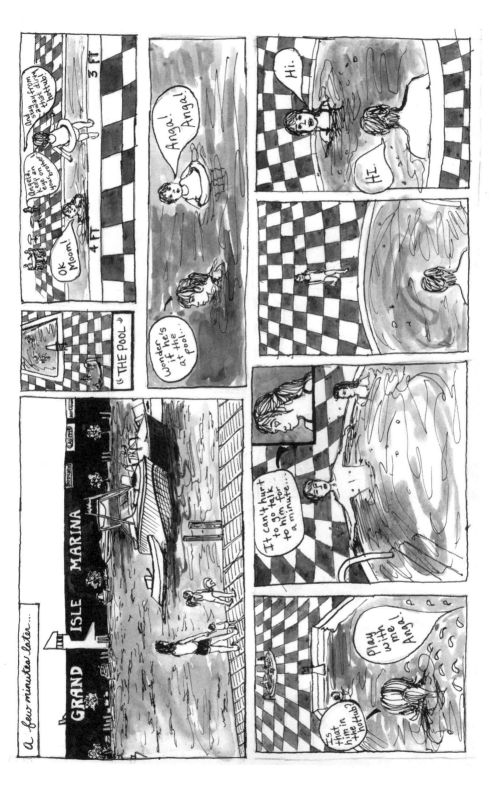

173

I Got My Mind Set On You • Angela Stork

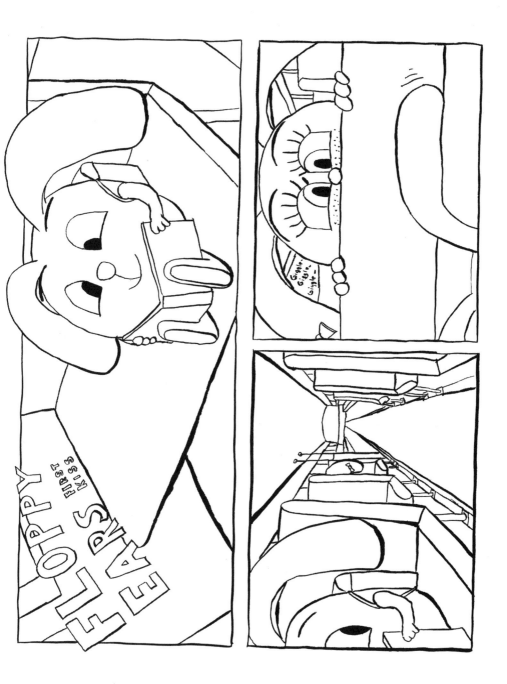

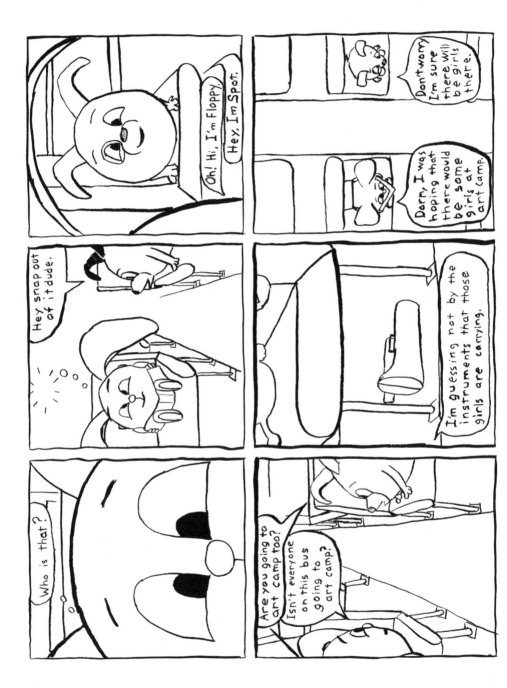

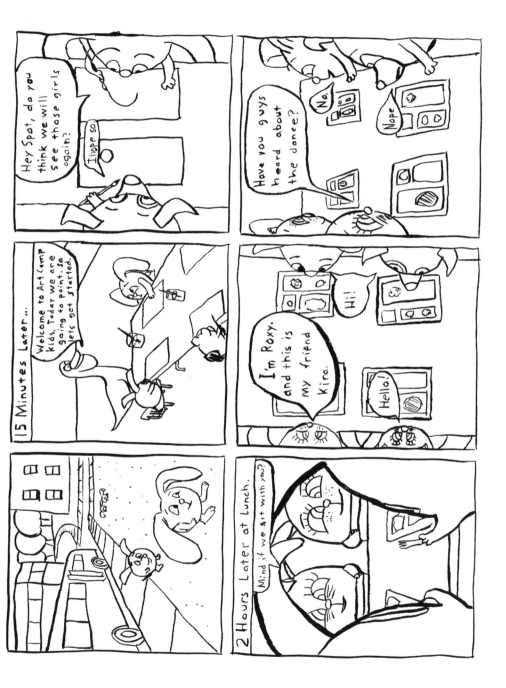

177

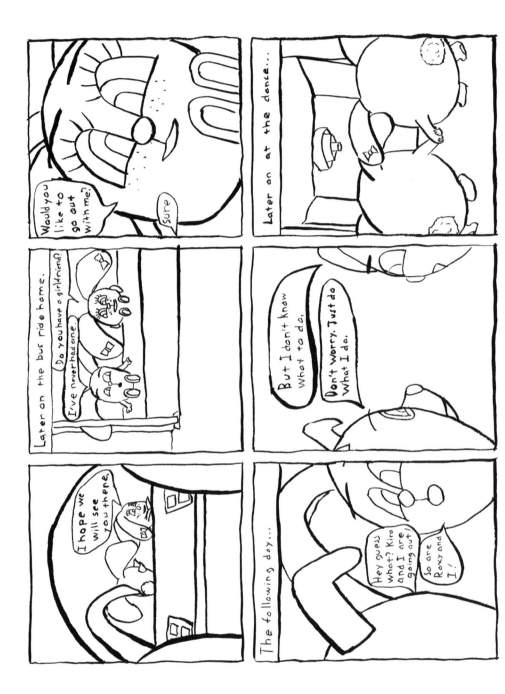

Floppy Ears' First Kiss • Dave Polk

Camp Lakeland • Karen Aronoff

183

Sometimes You Don't Realize • Sarah Sutton

Sometimes You Don't Realize • Sarah Sutton

Sometimes You Don't Realize • Sarah Sutton

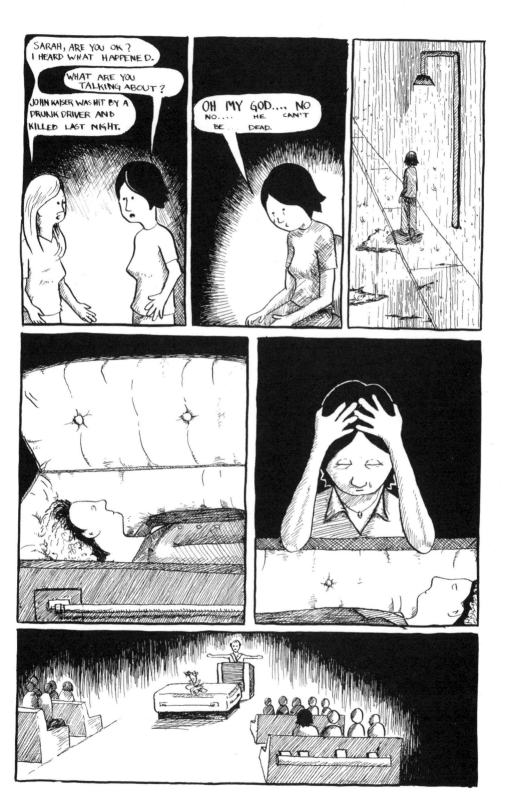

189

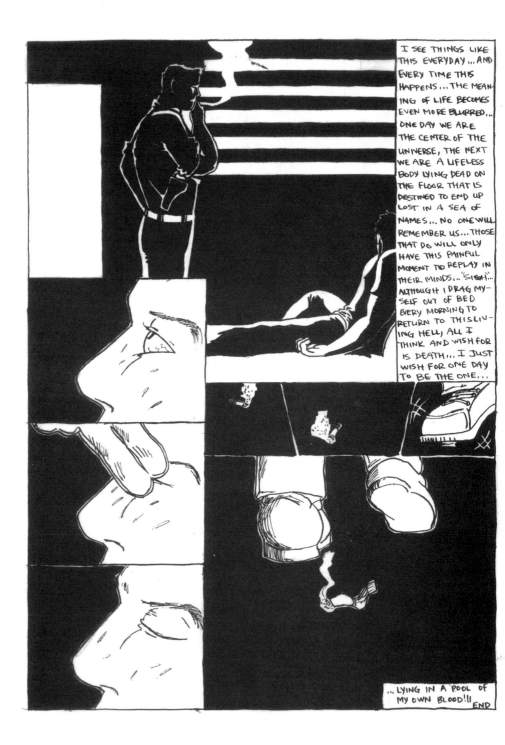

I SEE THINGS LIKE THIS EVERYDAY... AND EVERY TIME THIS HAPPENS... THE MEANING OF LIFE BECOMES EVEN MORE BLURRED... ONE DAY WE ARE THE CENTER OF THE UNIVERSE, THE NEXT WE ARE A LIFELESS BODY LYING DEAD ON THE FLOOR THAT IS DESTINED TO END UP LOST IN A SEA OF NAMES... NO ONE WILL REMEMBER US... THOSE THAT DO WILL ONLY HAVE THIS PAINFUL MOMENT TO REPLAY IN THEIR MINDS... "SIGH"... ALTHOUGH I DRAG MYSELF OUT OF BED EVERY MORNING TO RETURN TO THIS LIVING HELL, ALL I THINK AND WISH FOR IS DEATH... I JUST WISH FOR ONE DAY TO BE THE ONE...

... LYING IN A POOL OF MY OWN BLOOD!!! END

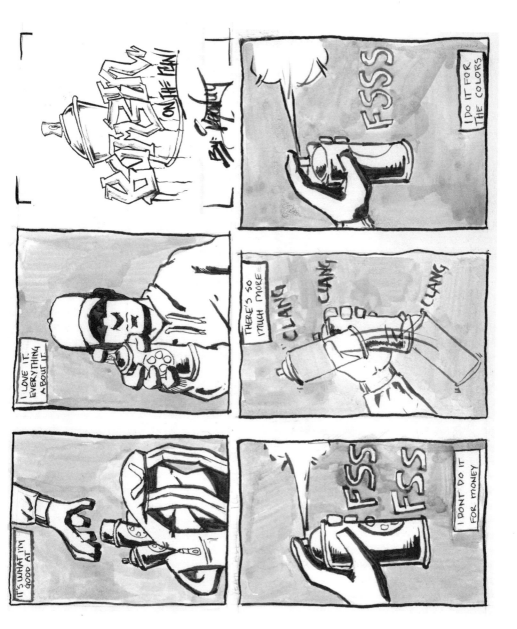

197

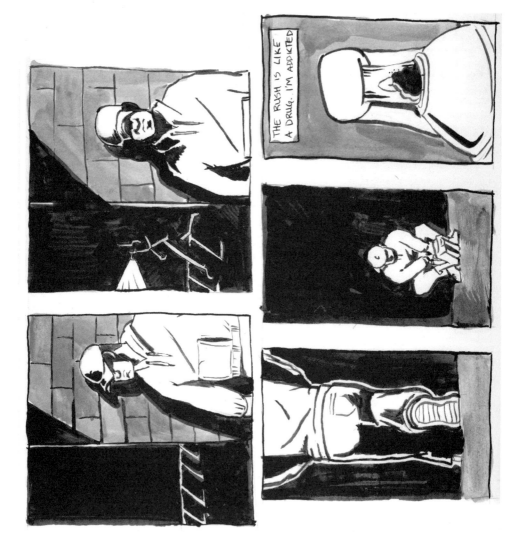

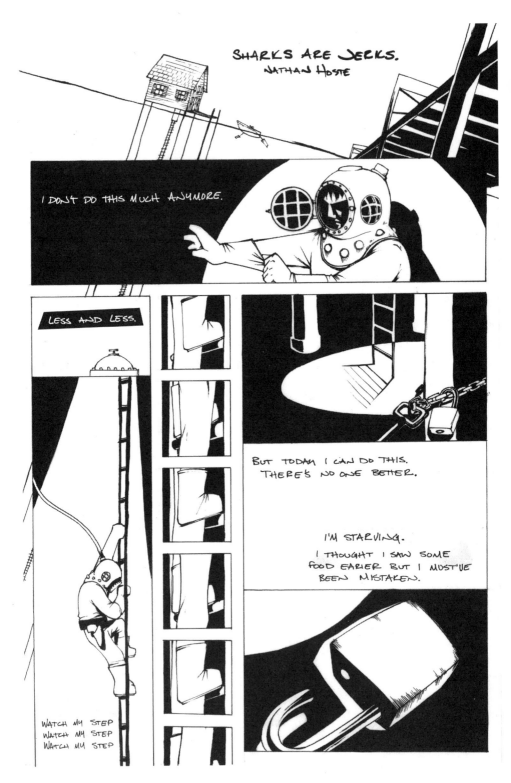

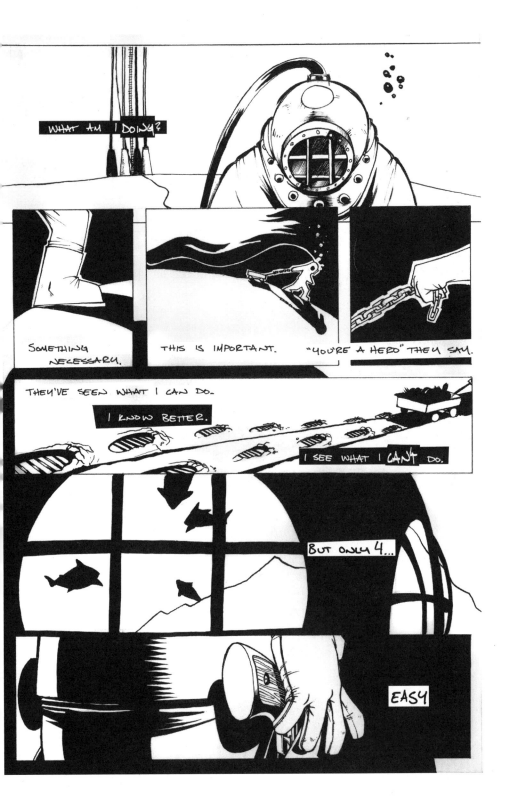

Sharks Are Jerks • Nathan Hoste

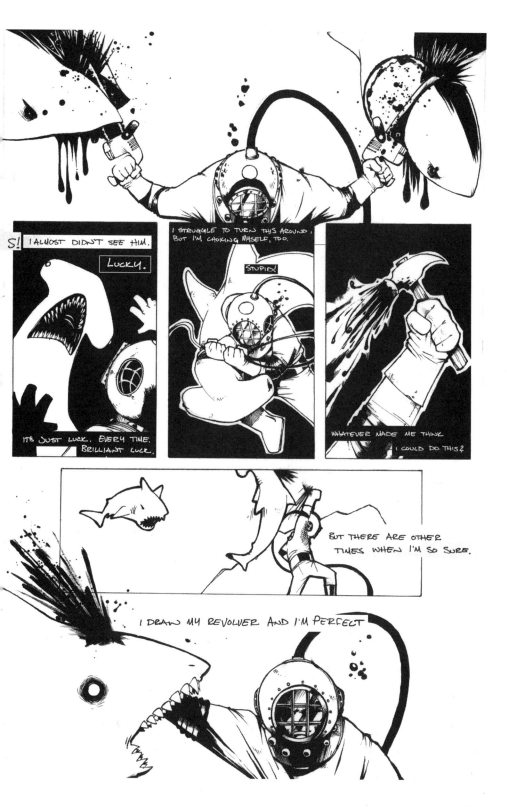

Sharks Are Jerks • Nathan Hoste

THE ACCIDENT IS A
FATAL ACCIDENT.
BUT IT'S OK.

NO ONE EVER SAW ME

FAIL.

Squishy Love • Cristina Mezuk

Squishy Love • Cristina Mezuk

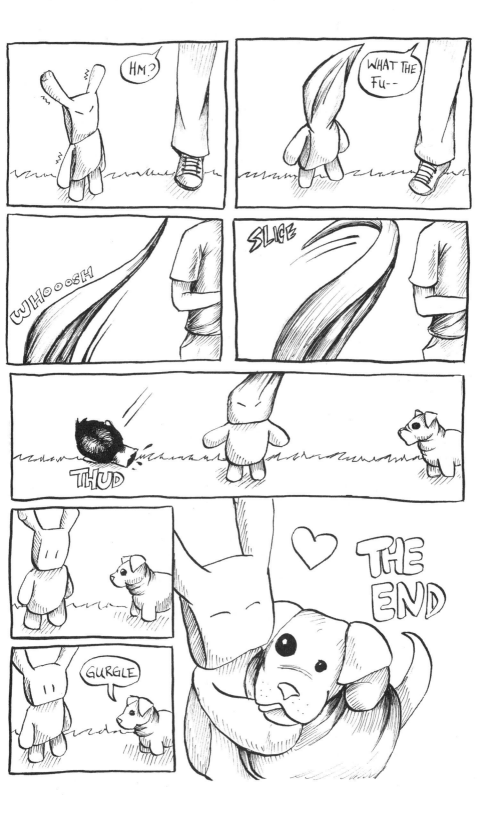

The Keeper • Joshua Johnson

The Keeper • Joshua Johnson

215

The Keeper • Joshua Johnson

The Manticore • Matt Merriweather

The Manticore • Matt Merriweather

3

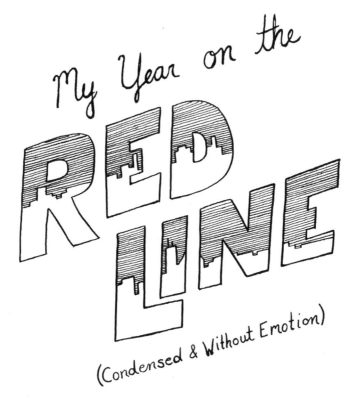

My Year on the **RED LINE** (Condensed & Without Emotion)

by Casey

WHEN I FIRST MOVED TO CHICAGO, I WAS TOTALLY NAIVE. I MOVED IN WITH TWO STRANGERS, DIDN'T HAVE A JOB, AND KNEW NEXT TO NOTHING ABOUT THE CITY. SO, NATURALLY, I HAD NO CLUE WHAT THE PUBLIC TRANSPORTATION WOULD BE LIKE . . . .

I WAS IN FOR A REAL TREAT

I HAD TO RELY ON THE "L" (ELEVATED SUBWAY SYSTEM) TO GET EVERYWHERE.

ON MY VERY FIRST RIDE, THERE WAS A POWER FAILURE.

THEY STOPPED ALL OF THE RED LINE TRAINS AND MADE US FIND OUR OWN WAY HOME.

I HAD NO IDEA WHERE I WAS.

CAN YOU TELL ME WHERE THE BUS STOP IS?

Casey Brooks • My Year On The Red Line

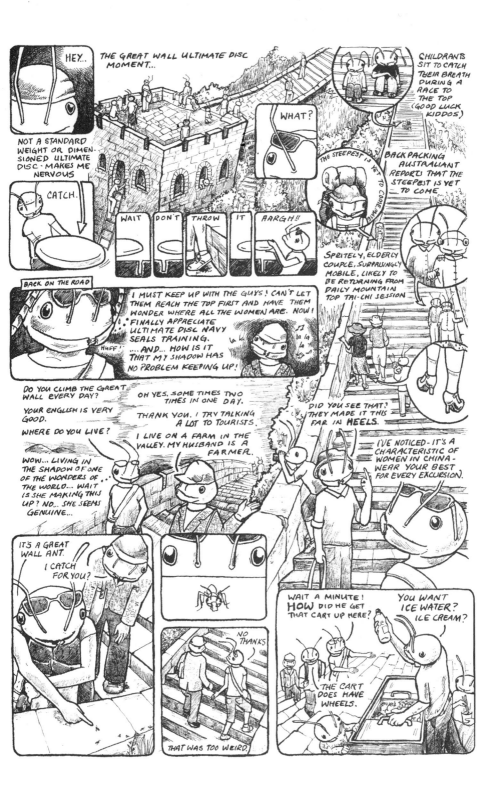

The Reality of Dylan Roberts • Jessica Yurasek

Hitler also gave him the St. James version of the Holy Bible.

... rule #3: Drink chocolate milk every day because it is free from sin. It can save you from corruption.

Hello there Mr. Squirrel. Are you hungry?

He told me other things Hitler taught him. Like how to chain smoke.

Or use a machete.

Or make omelets with cheese and mushrooms.

Dylan Robert loves to hide from reality. What a game he has constructed.

Hitler convinced him that some ancient animal instinct was controlling his mind and that as a direct result, the squirrels could understand him when he spoke.

The Reality of Dylan Roberts • Jessica Yurasek

WTF? • Brian Walline

WTF? • Brian Walline

Alisa Bischoff • Paper Cuts Back

~ 3 ~

The Reality of Dylan Rohrer by Jessica Naruseki

PIP SQUEAK

SOL

artists

... listed in no particular order.

JESSICA YURASEK Ultimately, I play two roles in life: a traveler and an artist. My journeys in both mediums have taught me a multitude of lessons, the greatest of which is that whatever we are as individuals, we are first humans and have an obligation to a greater good. I create because to do so is human, and art is truth. As an artist, it is my prerogative to share truth and beauty. By December 2004, I will have earned a double BFA in photography and graphic design, with a minor in art history from the University of Michigan School of Art and Design.

GEOFFREY SILVERSTEIN is a young artist and designer from St.Louis Missouri. For more information about his work visit www.geoffreysilverstein.com

JESSIE HOWELL is a graduating Senior at the Univesity of Michigan with a joint degree in Asian Studies and Painting. She was born in Detriot and grew up in Grand Rapids, Michigan. She doesn't talk much. Aside form comics, she enjoys reading Chinese literature and drinking beer. Next year she plans to spend a year teaching English in Shenzhen, China.

SARAH SUTTON was born to a conservative republican father and a democratic liberal mother. Growing up Sarah was torn between being a daddy's girl and his mother's ideals. She entered into the University of michigan's school of art and design as a bright eyed and bushy tailed freshman in 2001. Within the four years of college she met and became engaged to a fabulous young lady. She was disowned from her grandparents, but is happy with with her partner. Sarah is a happy little designer and loves to draw and has found an outlet for her drawing by creating comic books.

CRISTINA MEZUK At a very early age I had made up my mind to become an actress. However, after a horrible freak accident in a 6th grade play, my second choice of career become more prominent: art. I had been a big illustrator my whole life, just drawing little things for myself or other people. I picked up my first comic book in a creepy, random store on Leonard street in Grand Rapids, Michigan in 1993. Ever since then, I've been infatuated with comic books, and everything about them. In school I was always regarded as the weirdo-freak girl who enjoyed doing "boy stuff" and had a dark sense of humor, but that's just me. I decided to join the rest of the freaks and go to an art school to continue my love of comics.

LIA YOON-HONG MIN was born in 1983 (Akron, OH). She moved to Korea 1989 and moved back to the US 1999. She presently attends University of Michigan, pursuing MDDP in Fine Arts and Biology and minoring in Asian Studies. As for her future, who knows....
Graduate 2007 - Go to Graduate School - Get job (?) - Live and Die.
Her interests include small, soft, warm, and cute stuff, things that smell nice, delicacies, simplicity (like physics and numbers).

WARNER KING WASHINGTON II Born to Vickie Norman and Warner K. Washington I, I spent my formative childhood years in the outskirts of the city of Detroit. What made me pick up a pencil and start to draw when I was younger was definitely comics. So, in general, telling a story or giving my opinion of society through sequential art is one of my favorite things to do. I know comics can seem juvenile on the surface, but I feel like it is truly a fine way to tell stories or give your opinion.

MAX MOLLHAGEN-JAKSA (Jack McMacksaw) I grew up drawing and eating for the most part. As a child, my diet was primarily composed of Ritz crackers and Lifesavers. During this period of my life I was fatter and blonde. You could chalk up the fatness to the poor diet, but I was born at nearly 12 pounds, so genetics must've fit into the game at some point. I was also quite stationary. Blonde, fat, stationary. This led to wonderful career in drawing. Today my hair is brown, I am less fat, and still I am in great need of regular exercise. Still drawing though. In the future, I imagine grandchildren, decent hair, and a missing left arm. Lost it in a war, or car crash or something like that

ZACH TAKENAGA strives to produce art in a variety of fields, including filmmaking, painting, comic illustration, and music. He is currently a graduate of the University of Michigan, and looking to find his place in the world.

JONATHAN YUNG-HSIN HO was born in Taiwan. After 7 years, he and his family moved to the United States. In Livonia, MI, the whitest city in America, he spent crucial formulative years. Growing up in such a homogeneous environment had a devastating impact on his growth as a person. His eyes opened when, upon high school graduation, he made his way to the diverse city of Ann Arbor.) Jonathan spent five years at the U of M pursuing degrees in Mechanical Engineering and English Literature while occasionally sneaking into classes in the art school.

KRISTIN BUCKLESS is originally from Houston, Texas; the land of football, cheerleading and cowboy hats. As a child she was forbidden to partake in cheerleading so instead she found interest in sports, especially softball and volleyball where spandex shorts took the place of mini skirts. At the age of 2, she moved to Brighton, MI, the town known for its "Mountain" composed of a giant garbage heap. In her spare time she enjoys illustration, out door activities, traveling and watching any series on HBO. She hopes to bring humor to her art, believing laughter is the cure for everything at least for a moment in time.

KEVIN O'NEILL is a 21 year old who watches entirely too many movies to be considered to be in sound mental health. He also has a habit of trying to annoy his teachers via methods so subtle and nefarious that they fail entirely. He is most well known for creating pictures of things hitting other things. He also shares a name with a more famous comic artist, which has been mentioned prominently in audiences of up to one person.

MEGHAN JONIEC I am a senior in Graphic Design and as of April 30th, 2005 I will enter the world armed with my BFA from the University of Michigan. Advanced Illustration was a great class that helped me streamline my creative process. Hope you like.

ALISA BISCHOFF is from Tawas, Michigan. After moving to Arizona, Washington, Utah, Colorado, and New York City, she now lives, works, and misbehaves in general in Ann Arbor. Although she is graduating in August 2005 with a major in Graphic Design, she plans on continuing to draw comics until she is permanently disabled by carpal tunnel syndrome (so that means...for a very long time.)
Alisa designed this book!

ALEXIS JAKOBSON is an art student at the University of Michigan. She likes: mini sharpies, creative cropping, hotel room paintings.

KELLY CAMPBELL Raised in southeastern Indiana a long, long time ago, I have always been fascinated by cars, especially hot rods and customs. Flames always seemed to be the essence of rebellion to me. It has been a lifelong dream to have a car with flames on it; Indiana, however, was not really an area where the car was idolized as it is in Detroit. It was the Woodward Dream Cruise in 1996 that really opened my eyes to the excitement of "car culture". Combine the Dream Cruise, the Art Car Parade in Houston, four years living near the "Motor City", a desire to create public art, and the Route 66 truck was born

JEREMY STOLL is a writer, artist, activist, student, and many other things. He currently resides in Ann Arbor, MI, but will be attending the University of Indiana's Graduate Program in Folklore in the Fall of 2005. He has been drawing comics since his sophomore year in college, when a friend urged him to put the fictional characters he drew constantly into a narrative form. His first comic sucked. After that, things could only look up, and hopefully what is here presented is better.

PATRICK ECKHOLD I came to U of M in 2000, and am still currently trying to complete a joint degree of Biological Psychology and Scientific Illustration. It is a slow, long and arduous process. I have always been interested in drawing and have also been fascinated by comics. My interest in psychology has directed the comics that I have created so far. They all seem to have some weird hallucinogenic and psychedelic twist on them, which do not necessarily reflect any personal demons, but instead allow me the freedom that I think I need as a starting cartoonist to freely express whatever wacky idea comes to mind.

BRUCE BRENNEISE was born and raised in a cult in rural Michigan. Escaping from that life when sixteen, he has developed a revulsion for vegetarian hotdogs and dreads the advent of the seventh day of the week. He had always believed that someday he would be an author, but due to the vagaries of fate he somehow became a student of fine arts. Based on a dissection of time spent during college, he might also be striving for minors in Horror fiction, Instant Messenger addiction, and spilt milk. Hopefully these pursuits will serve him well in his soon-to-be professional life as a world traveler, night owl, and unapologetic bum.

BROOKE WRIGHT went to the cupboard to get her poor class a short bio.
But when she got there, she found flour, eggs, and cheese; and so her poor
class got cheese puffs instead.

DAVID TESNAR I am the youngest of six children. Being the youngest surely has its advantages, but when the parents are gone it is the exact opposite. Having 4 older brothers and 1 sister begins to make its mark on a kid as he is locked in the hamper or pushed down the stairs in a diaper box. However, I would not have it any other way, now that I am bigger than most of the them. I attribute my interest in the graphic arts to admiration of what my older siblings did as artists. My love for drawing as a cartoonist is an easy transition from my quirky sense of humor in design. This humor is not something that just comes to me, but rather derived from all of the re-occurring weird experiences in my day-to-day life.

THEA HOCKIN

Born: 1979

Died:

Likes: comic books, tacos

Dislikes: chili, bad guys

ANGELA STORK Influenced by THE LITTLE MERMAID, young Angela Stork wanted to draw for Disney when she grew up. Now she is three months away from graduation and she worries about it on a constant basis. She would be ecstatic to become a writer and illustrator of books, but is thinking of applying to graduate school for museum studies so she may have a more lucrative career. Outside of painting and drawing, Angela enjoys casual glasses of wine, snowboarding, HBO series, english classes, walks in the Arb, and Adult Swim before bed.

DAVE POLK Born in Missouri. Grew up in Michigan. Learned to like art from his grandmother. Continued to take art classes growing up. Graduated with a B.F.A. from the University of Michigan.

KEREN ARONOFF grew up in Amherst, New York, right outside of Buffalo. She is a an of camp, traveling, music, film, recording, constructing, editing, and laughing. She aspires to produce significant and creative work in her lifetime.

KOU YANG was born in New Jersey but now resides in Detroit, MI. He has five sisters and one brother. He currently works for the Evigna Corporation in Troy, MI. He is a part time student studying mechanical engineering and industrial design at the University of Michigan. His favorite comic books are the Amazing Spiderman and Astonishing X-Men; his favorite artists are Jim Lee and John Cassaday.

KOON NGUY The name's Koon. I love comics. Alot. Reading, Writing, and Illustrating... all of it.

NATHAN HOSTE was born the day after the Tigers won the World Series in 1984. He draws pictures. He probably wouldn't like you, but there's still that slim chance.

HENRY ADAM DOUGHERTY was born in Bryn Mawr, Pennsylvania where so far he has spent most of his life. Superhero comic books first sparked his imagination in illustration during his years in lower school and have continued to influence his work ever since. Henry is now a senior at the University of Michigan, where he studies graphic design with a minor in art history. He intends to continue his work back in Pennsylvania after college with the intentions continuing his work in illustration. NOTE: due to a technical glitch, you'll have to look for Adam's story in next yeear's book. But he's here in spirit.

JOSH JOHNSON was born in Ypsilanti, MI. His Education Includes: Willow Run High(The Run), Washtenaw Community College,and University of Michigan's School of Art & Design. Josh completed his first children's book in the summer of 2005, "When A Kid Dreams" compliments of Zoe' Life Publishing. He enjoys to write and illustrate for children of all ages.

MATT MERRIWEATHER is from West Bloomfield, Michigan. He has been drawing and writing comics since high school, which is where he created his character "The Flying Tomato."

MINDY STEFFEN has loved to draw cartoons since childhood, featuring her dogs and Sonic the Hedgehog. Her favorite season is spring and favorite ice cream is chocolate chip cookie dough. Currently, she has many characters that scream to escape her head onto the press (or TV???). She has dillusions of grandeur, but at least she can try....

CASEY BROOKS uses elbow grease. She recently returned to school after 2 years away, and is focusing on painting with a little printmaking on the side. She also sells her work out of vending machines.

JENNIFER ZEE I was born in Los Angeles and grew up in Hong Kong, where I spent my days hanging out with my dog (a hyperactive boxer named Poopy), playing with insects (picture giant grasshoppers in tutus fashioned out of Kleenex), and drawing a lot. Convinced that I wanted to dedicate my life to studying biology of the ecology and evolutionary biology sort, I made it to a biology graduate program, where I studied Argentine ant raiding behavior on other ants (not for the faint-hearted! Ant mutilations were a common outcome). I realized that I did not want to be known as ant-lady for the rest of my life, so I answered to my true calling and applied to art schools. Being referred to as ant-lady in an artistic sense is acceptable.

SAM BUTLER Raised in Royal Oak, Michigan, Sam Butler is an Art major with minors in Art History and Political Science; and the answer is no – he doesn't know what he's going to do with those degrees either. During his four years at the University of Michigan, Sam worked for the student newspaper and has won several awards for his published editorial cartoons. Exemplified by this experience, Sam greatly enjoys both drawing and writing, however he abhors writing autobiographical blurbs.

JIM GIANPETRO My childhood was spent like many suburban boys, years whizzing by playing various sports and getting into the occasional mischief. Something I remember doing and enjoying even before sports is drawing. My parents kept a box of paper in the coffee table for my creative convenience as a child. I was constantly drawing. There's a certain pleasure I get through drawing, but that same kind of pleasure has now been manifested in my love for design. Now that I have explored graphic design, it has become my new passion. I feel extremely lucky to have the chance to pursue something I simply love to do.

BRIAN WALLINE I've been drawing for as long as anyone can remember but it wasn't until I recognized the impulse to craft every visual manifestation of my high school cross country team in the image of my own taste that I identified design as a true passion. After four years of living in front of a computer this effort represents a renewed dedication to drawing for me, although I'm sure my 7th grade classmates would be distraught over the lack of superheroes. Other interests include bourbon, space elevators, and being the poet laureate of a dirty arch street basement.

PROFESSOR PHOEBE GLOECKNER is a graphic novelist, the author of **A Child's Life and Other Stories** and **The Diary of a Teenage Girl**. She's the teacher, and that's why her picture is slightly larger than those preceding it. I'd like to note that the larger picture is better balanced with the imploring earnestness expressed in the portrait of the student directly above her. She's been an assistant professor at The University of Michigan for one year.

264

thanks

JUSTIN GREEN is a legendary cartoonist, the author of the 1973 masterpiece, **Binky Brown Meets the Holy Virgin Mary.** The Fall 2004 class was privileged to meet Mr. Green face-to-face when he came to Ann Arbor in a rare appearance as visiting artist/ guest lecturer in December. Not only did he bring his drawing table all the way from Cincinnatti, but he left each student with a gift-- a piece of marble to wipe their pens on, and a special antique pen nib!
• **lecture documented on video.**

BILL GRIFFITH and DIANE NOOMIN are arguably two of the most influential figures in comics today. They were Penny Stamps lecturers in February and then came and spoke more about their work in our Winter 2005 class. Bill Griffith is the creator of **Zippy the Pinhead,** a nationally syndicated strip, and Diane Noomin is the creator of the character **Didi Glitz** as well as the editor of many books, including **Wimmin's Comics, Arcade,** and the ground-breaking 1990s anthology, **Twisted Sisters.**
• **lecture documented on video.**

RICHARD RUBENFELD is Professor of History at Eastern Michigan University in Ypsilanti. He was the curator of **Holey Moley!,** an exhibiton of original comic art at EMU last fall. Artists represented in the show included Windsor McCay, George Herriman, Bill Day, and many others. The Fall class went on a field trip to see this inspiring show and to hear a fascinating lecture given by Dr. Rubenfeld. It is not often that one has the opportunity to see great original comics drawings up close.

LYDIA GREGG and KARL KRESSBACH are now both U of M alumnae. While students in the School of Art and Design, they collaborated in the production of a comix tabloid magazine, **HOAX.** This Spring, **HOAX** graduated to bi-annual status and is now available to the retail market through Diamond Distribuors. Lydia and Karl graced us once each semester with presentations and discussions of their ambitious, spooky, wildly original art.

ANNETTE HAINES is The School of Art and Design's Field Librarian. She was instrumental in aquiring many new graphic novels and comic books for the Art, Architecture, and Engineering Library, as well as in processing the many generous donations of books the School has received. She also accompanied Professor Gloeckner to **Le Festival International de la Bande Dessinée** in Angoulême, France, in January. Here she is having breakfast at the home of R. Crumb and Aline Kominsky. No joke.

THANKS also to Bryan Rogers, Dean of The School of Art and Design, Mahendra Kumar in the finance office, Professor Patricia Olynyk, and Bill Gosling, University Librarian.

Questions and comments are welcomed.
If you wish to contact the editor
or one of the artists,
please visit woodenbook.org